GERALDINE COTTER'S
SEINN AN PIANO

PLAYING THE PIANO
～ IRISH STYLE ～

OSSIAN

This tutor is dedicated to my parents Dympna and Eddie Cotter.
Mam was my first piano teacher and along with Dad
gave me every support and encouragement.

Acknowledgements

© 1996, Geraldine Cotter
© 1996, Ossian Publications Co. Ltd
   World Copyright

All rights reserved, including the right of reproduction in
whole or in part in any form or by any means without the
prior permission of the copyright owners. Photocopying
any part of this work is illegal and expressly forbidden by
the Copyright Act of 1956.
Copying is also illogical and short-sighted, as because of it,
authors, composers and arrangers will not receive royalties
for their work, nor will the publishers be able to continue
their job of producing new titles.

Continuity, layout and typesetting by Grace O'Halloran
Music origination by Frances Hamilton and Claire O'Loughlin
Music correction by Frances Hamilton
Additional music correction by Grace O'Halloran
Original stained glass cover design by John Boyd.
Cover by Rob Mullins
Photo credits on page 74.

I would like to thank all those who helped me in producing this book,
including those who willingly supplied photos;
A special thanks to my husband John Boyd for his advice and help
and especially for the unique cover design;
Thanks also to the following: my family, Conor McCarthy, Reg Hall,
Charlie Harris, Paul Brock, Mícheál Ó Siochrú, Custy's Music Shop;
Andrew Robinson - Maoin Cheoil an Chláir;
Matt Purcell - Harmony Row Studios;
Harry Bradshaw and Nicholas Carolan - Irish Traditional Music Archive;
Mícheál Ó Súilleabháin, who proofread the manuscript and offered
many helpful suggestions;
A thank you also to my publisher John Loesberg and to all the staff
of Ossian Publications, especially Grace O'Halloran.

In conjunction with this book two demo-cassettes are available:

OSS 93 **Demo cassette**. This cassette contains all the techniques
and tunes described in chapters 1-3 in the book.
OSS 94 **Tune cassette**. Features all the tunes in the final chapter
of the book, first played slowly, then at speed.

Ossian Publications
P.O. Box 84, Cork, Ireland
e-mail: ossian@iol.ie

OMB 103   ISBN 0 946005 92 3

Contents

	Page
Preface	4
Introduction	5
Chapter 1	15
Chapter 2	18
Chapter 3	33
Chapter 4	47
Bibliography	71
Discography	72

PREFACE

I have written this book for the simple reason that there is not one available like it. The piano may not be a traditional instrument in the way the flute, fiddle, pipes or concertina are, however I see no reason why traditional Irish music should not be played on it. In the last number of years traditional music has become common on instruments with which fifty years ago it was not remotely associated.

I would like to make a point about the separateness of the vamping/accompaniment approach and the tune-playing approach. In the past the piano was mostly used to accompany music. It was very rarely used as a melodic instrument. One possible reason for this may be that traditional music was for the most part leaned without music and piano players, in general being classically trained, used notation. Most pianists who accompanied Irish music did so without notation. However, that is a topic of discussion for another time.

I have not presented this tutor in the usual sense of the word - I am not including the basic techniques of piano playing. The player attempting this book should have some years' experience.

I have dealt with topics such as solo piano playing and accompaniment. Chapter 1 gives a simple approach: tunes without ornamentation. I have included fingering in this chapter, which should help, particularly with the faster tunes. Chapter 2 introduces more difficult tunes and also the concepts of variation and ornamentation. Chapter 3 introduces vamping (accompanying Irish music).

Irish music is fundamentally an aural tradition, which means that there is no fixed way of playing any particular tune. Every musician will put his or her 'stamp' on a tune. The basic tune may sound the same but the ornamentation and variation will differ from player to player. The examples I have given are to be taken only as guidelines. There are many possibilities open to the player. Do not take my arrangements as the only correct ones. Use them as a springboard towards developing your own style. I have omitted all ornamentation in Chapter 4, to give you a chance to try it yourself.

The introduction, while detailed in some respects, is not a complete study. It serves to put into context the place of the piano in Irish traditional music.

I will conclude by saying that the usual rules of good piano playing apply. Correct posture at the piano, clarity and good intonation of notes are just as important for traditional playing as for any other music.

I hope that you find many hours of pleasure in working through this book. If this is your first introduction to Irish music maybe you will feel encouraged to find out more.

Geraldine Cotter, 1995.

Introduction

The Piano and Traditional Music

Publications

Despite the fact that the piano is considered to be a non-traditional instrument there are references to its use since the 18th century, when Edward Bunting published the first 'Ancient Music of Ireland' in 1796. The tunes in this book were collected at the Belfast Harp Festival, which was attended by a gathering of harpers including O'Carolan, Hempson and Rory Dall Ó Catháin. The airs were arranged by Bunting for the piano.

A later collection by George Petrie also contained airs arranged for the piano. This was called 'The Ancient Music of Ireland', published in 1855 for the Society for the Preservation and Publication of the Melodies of Ireland.

> THE
> ANCIENT MUSIC
> OF
> IRELAND.
> Arranged for the
> PIANO FORTE.
>
> To which is prefixed
> A DISSERTATION ON
> THE IRISH HARP AND HARPERS,
> INCLUDING AN ACCOUNT OF THE
> OLD MELODIES OF IRELAND.
>
> BY EDWARD BUNTING.
>
> Dublin:
> HODGES AND SMITH.
> 1840.

Bunting published almost 300 airs in the three collections of 1796, 1809 and 1840

Waifs and Strays of Gaelic Melody

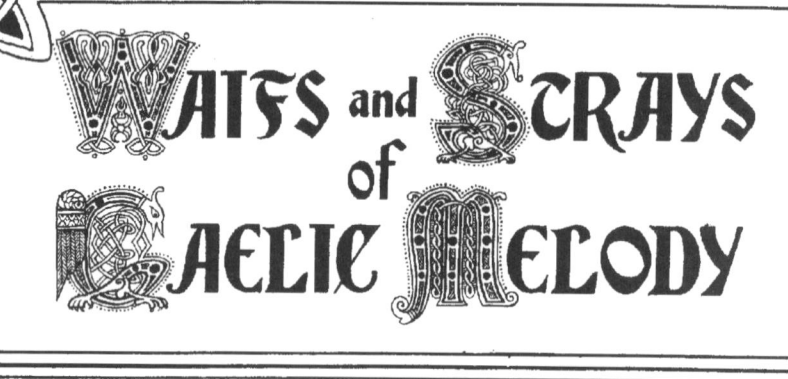

Comprising Forgotten Favorites, Worthy Variants, and Tunes not Previously Printed.

Collected and Edited by

Capt. Francis O'Neill

Compiler and Publisher of
"The Music of Ireland," "The Dance Music of Ireland,"
and "O'Neill's Irish Music for Piano or Violin."
AUTHOR OF
"Irish Folk Music – A Fascinating Hobby,"
and "Irish Minstrels and Musicians."

ARRANGED BY
Selena O'Neill, Mus.Bac.

In the 1920s Captain Francis O'Neill published 'Waifs and Strays of Gaelic Melody'. The tunes in this collection were arranged for piano by Selena O'Neill (no relation).

SELENA O'NEILL

Waltons of Dublin were involved in numerous publications for piano including 3 'Volumes of Irish Music' arranged by T.M. Crofts; and 'The Dance Music of Ireland' arranged by R.M. Levey.

Carl G. Hardebeck (1869-1945) was born in London and lived in Ireland from 1893. Although blind from infancy he collected and transcribed Irish music by adapting the braille system to suit the Irish alphabet. He arranged many of these airs for piano.

Publications in America included 'Dance Music of Ireland' by John J. Ward. In 1971 Ed Reavy published his own compositions in a volume called 'Where the Shannon Rises' which contained chordal accompaniment.

Charlie Lennon's book 'Musical Memories' contains his own compositions, with written accompaniment for piano.

RECORDINGS

Recordings have been made of traditional Irish music for the piano since the 1920s. During the early part of this century many thousands of Irish traditional musicians lived in the U.S. Recordings of players such as Michael Coleman, James Morrison, Paddy Killoran, William Mulally, John McKenna and the Flanagan brothers all had piano accompaniment. These pianists included Clare Reardon, Ed Geoghegan, Eileen O'Shea, Seán Frain, Charles Bender, Della McMahon, Paddy Muldoon, Frank Fallon, A.P. Kenna and Ed Lee (a brother of Frank Lee in London). In Boston John O'Connell recorded with Joe Derrane in the 1940s and 1950s. In New York Alex Browne played with Martin Byrne's 'Irish Blackbird Orchestra' in the 1930s. Non-Irish Players such as Tom Banks, John Muller and Joe Linder also accompanied Irish music. Accompanists had to be members of the musicians' union in order to record.

BOX PLAYER JOHN KIMMEL
ACCOMPANIED BY
JOE LINDER ON PIANO.

In the 1920s and 1930s, several solo piano recordings were made by Dan Sullivan, leader of the Shamrock Band and son of Dan Sullivan the fiddle player from Kerry. A salesman for Steinway pianos in Boston, he recorded two 78s of reels and airs. He influenced many piano players with his lively style. Other great piano solos were recorded by Eleanor Kane in the 1930s. She lived in Chicago and was regarded highly both as a soloist and accompanist. She played with many musicians including Paddy Killoran. Musician and composer Ed Reavy composed a reel in her honour.

ED REAVY

One of the finest piano players I've heard was Bridie Lafferty who played with the Castle Céilí Band, Joe Cooley, and also accompanied on one of my favourite albums 'All Ireland Champions' with Peter O'Loughlin, Paddy Canny, and P.J. Hayes. (See Discography)
She also played solo piano but to my knowledge there are no recordings of this available.

PIANO PLAYER BRIDIE LAFFERTY

Recordings of traditional music continued and in the 1950s some fine piano playing was recorded by Josephine Keegan accompanying Seán Maguire. Maguire was also accompanied by Seán O'Driscoll in 1949 and later by Eileen Lane. More great piano playing can be heard on the album 'Ceol Tíre' with pianists Moya Acheson, Mrs. O'Connor and Brendan Mac Eachrain. This great album was produced by Comhaltas Ceoltóirí Éireann.

KINCORA CÉILÍ BAND WITH MRS. K. O'CONNOR ON PIANO

One of the best live recordings ever made was in 1967 in a London pub called the Favourite. The recording features some of the finest emigrant musicians of the time. Musicians such as Bobby Casey, Tony McMahon, Lucy Farr, Jimmy Power, Con Curtin, Julia Clifford, Danny Meehan, John O'Shea and Máirtín Byrnes all play to the accompaniment of Reg Hall on the piano.

JIMMY POWER (FIDDLE), TONY LEDWITH (ACCORDION), WITH REG HALL ON PIANO

Many of these recordings were made abroad and sent or brought home to Ireland by emigrants, where they influenced generations of musicians.

Some 78 labels:

JAMES MORRISON, (FIDDLE)
TOM ENNIS (PIPES)
JOHN MULLER (PIANO)
APRIL 1923

FRANK LEE'S
TARA CÉILÍ BAND

9

Céilí Bands

Musicians have always played together in groups. However a number of things occurred in the 1920s which eventually led to the line-up of the Céilí Band as we now know it. The availability of 78 recordings, including those brought home by emigrants, the opening of commercial dance halls, and the foundation of radio broadcasting through 2RN on New Year's Day 1926, all influenced this development. In fact on the opening night of 2RN the Dick Smith Trio became the first traditional group to broadcast.

In the 1930s the London-based Tara Céilí Band with piano player Frank Lee, a brother of Ed Lee mentioned earlier, recorded in Dublin and London. Their line up was fiddle, flute/piccolo, piano accordion, backed up by piano and drums.

As mentioned earlier, there was much interest in group music in the U.S. as is evident from the number of recordings made. Because of the increase in emigration from Ireland the demand for larger venues grew which in turn led to bigger groups of musicians. More formality in dress and in performance was demanded. This formality was also evident in performances broadcast on radio. Ed Lee's Four Provinces Orchestra, Dan Sullivan's Shamrock Band, O'Leary's Irish Minstrels, were among the many U.S. bands popular in the 1920s and 30s.

FRANK LEE

In Ireland dancing took place in houses or at the crossroads on platforms until the Dance Hall Act of 1935 required that all public dances be licensed. This ended the tradition, which became illegal as a result of the act. Consequently, the Céilí Band developed and became very popular.

THE BALLINAKILL CÉILÍ BAND WITH ANNA RAFFERTY ON PIANO, C. 1926

In 1926 Father Larkin, a curate in Ballinakill, Co. Galway, organised a group of five musicians including pianist Anna Rafferty, Stephen Moloney, Tommy Whyte, Gerry Moloney and Tommy Whelan. They played locally for a few years and in 1928 performed at a feis in Athlone. There they met Séamus Clandillon, the Director of 2RN, the first Irish Broadcasting Station. He broadcast them live in November 1929. In 1938 the group travelled to London to record a session. While not a band in the usual sense, the group led to a second generation Ballinakill Band formed by Tommy Whyte's daughter Aggie.

MANUSCRIPT GIVEN TO ANNA RAFFERTY BY FATHER LARKIN.

(Source: 'Irish Dance Music' - Folkways Records FW8821)

In Clare the two most dominant bands evolved in much the same way. In Kilfenora a group of musicians gathered to raise funds for the local church in 1907. This tradition carried on and eventually led to the famous band of the 1950s. The renowned piano player Kitty Linnane, who died in 1993, contributed greatly to the unique sound of this band.

THE KILFENORA CÉILÍ BAND OF THE 1950S.

There were many groupings of musicians in East Clare but the Tulla Band proper was formed by piano player Teresa Tubridy to compete at Féile Luimní in 1946. At a later stage Séan Reid (who died in the early 1970s) replaced Teresa Tubridy on piano. More recently George Byrt played with them. Ann Larkin, Pat Corry and I also had short stints with the band.

THE TULLA CÉILÍ BAND OF THE 1950S WITH SEÁN REID ON PIANO.

During the 1950s the Kilfenora and Tulla Bands dominated the Band scene in Clare. Other popular bands of the time included the Laichtín Naofa Céilí Band from Miltown Malbay, the Fiach Rua band from Kilmaley, Co. Clare and the Aughrim Slopes Band from Co. Galway.
During the 1950s and 1960s, as Rock and Roll music became more accessible to the Irish people, the interest in Céilí Band music gradually lessened. However, with the renewed interest in set dancing, present day Céilí Bands are becoming increasingly popular. Some of today's most popular bands include the Shaskeen Céilí Band, the Moving Cloud (piano - Carl Hession), the Templehouse Céilí Band (piano by Mary Corcoran), and the new Kilfenora Céilí Band (winners of the All-Ireland Championship in 1993, '94 and '95 - piano played by Fintan McMahon). In London one of the most popular bands is the Thatch Céilí Band formed by Clareman Brendan Mulkere. The piano is played by Kevin Taylor, son of flute player Paddy Taylor from Limerick.

JIMMY GIBLIN, JOHNNY MCGREEVY, ANN SCULLY WITH ELEANOR KANE ON PIANO

More information is contained in Chapter 3 and in Discography and Bibliography paragraphs.

RECENT DEVELOPMENTS

In the 1960s, a new style of ensemble playing was evolved by Seán Ó Riada. He developed a new style of group music making which was for a listening audience in a concert hall setting. The result was the successful Ceoltóirí Cualainn. Ó Riada himself played the harpsichord with this group, having chosen this instrument because of its resemblance in sound to the old Irish harp. He repopularised traditional music and influenced countless musicians in his short life, including his son Peadar who is carrying on the tradition.

SEÁN Ó RIADA

Ceoltóirí Cualainn evolved to become the Chieftains. Their harpist, Derek Bell, occasionally doubles as a pianist for the group.
Mícheál Ó Súilleabháin (another musician who was influenced by Ó Riada) has broken new ground in presenting Irish music on the piano. Incorporating elements of jazz, blues and classical music into his compositions, he has arranged music for both jazz and orchestral groups. He has many recordings and compositions to his credit.

MICHEÁL Ó SÚILLEABHÁIN

A new development in piano accompaniment to Irish music stems from a Cape Breton influence. This style is very lively, with a very syncopated right hand and broken chords in the left hand. Donna Long's playing has this approach as has that of Máire O'Keeffe. There is no doubting the 'lift' in this style.
The use of keyboards is quite common among the traditional groups of recent times, as can be seen from the recordings of such groups as Arcady, The Bothy Band and Stockton's Wing. In fact many of today's more popular groups have used keyboards at one time or another. The list of recordings is excellent so it is safe to conclude that the piano's future as an accompanying instrument is secure.
The piano as a solo instrument is a different case altogether. With the exception of the recordings of Dan Sullivan and Eleanor Kane (mentioned earlier), and some by Patsy Broderick, Ó Riada's harpsichord recordings, and those of Mícheál Ó Súilleabháin, there have been few recordings of solo keyboard music. There are many possible reasons for this but perhaps that is a topic for another occasion.

Geraldine Cotter's seinn an Piano

CHAPTER 1

The tunes in this chapter are very simple ones accompanied by easy chords. I have written in the fingering to help you. As with all piano music, it is better to practise hands separately. Remember that in this music the left hand exists as an accompaniment. Don't worry about the speed of the tune until you've gained confidence playing slowly.

Kerry Polka

This polka is played for sets, mainly in Counties Kerry, Cork and Waterford. The first half is very easy, as you don't have to move your hand from its position. The second half is more difficult.

Tá'n Coileach ag Fógairt an Lae

This is in jig time (2 beats in the bar). Remember to practise hands separately at first. Take note of the fingering.

Nead na Lachan sa Mhúta

This is a slip jig (also called a hop jig). It's in 9/8 time (3 beats per bar). The main accent is on the first beat of the bar.

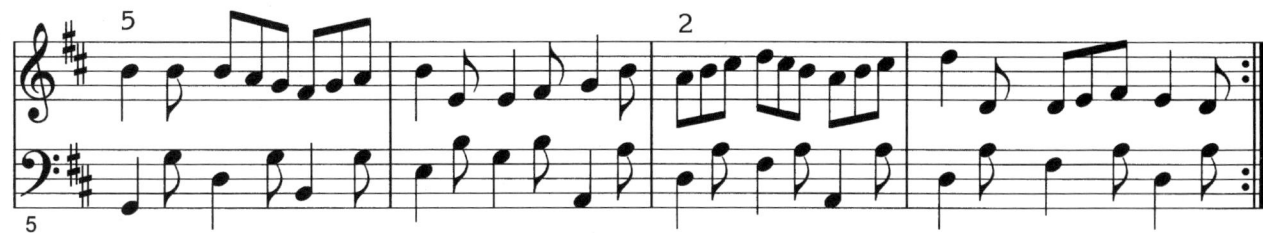

Lannigan's Ball

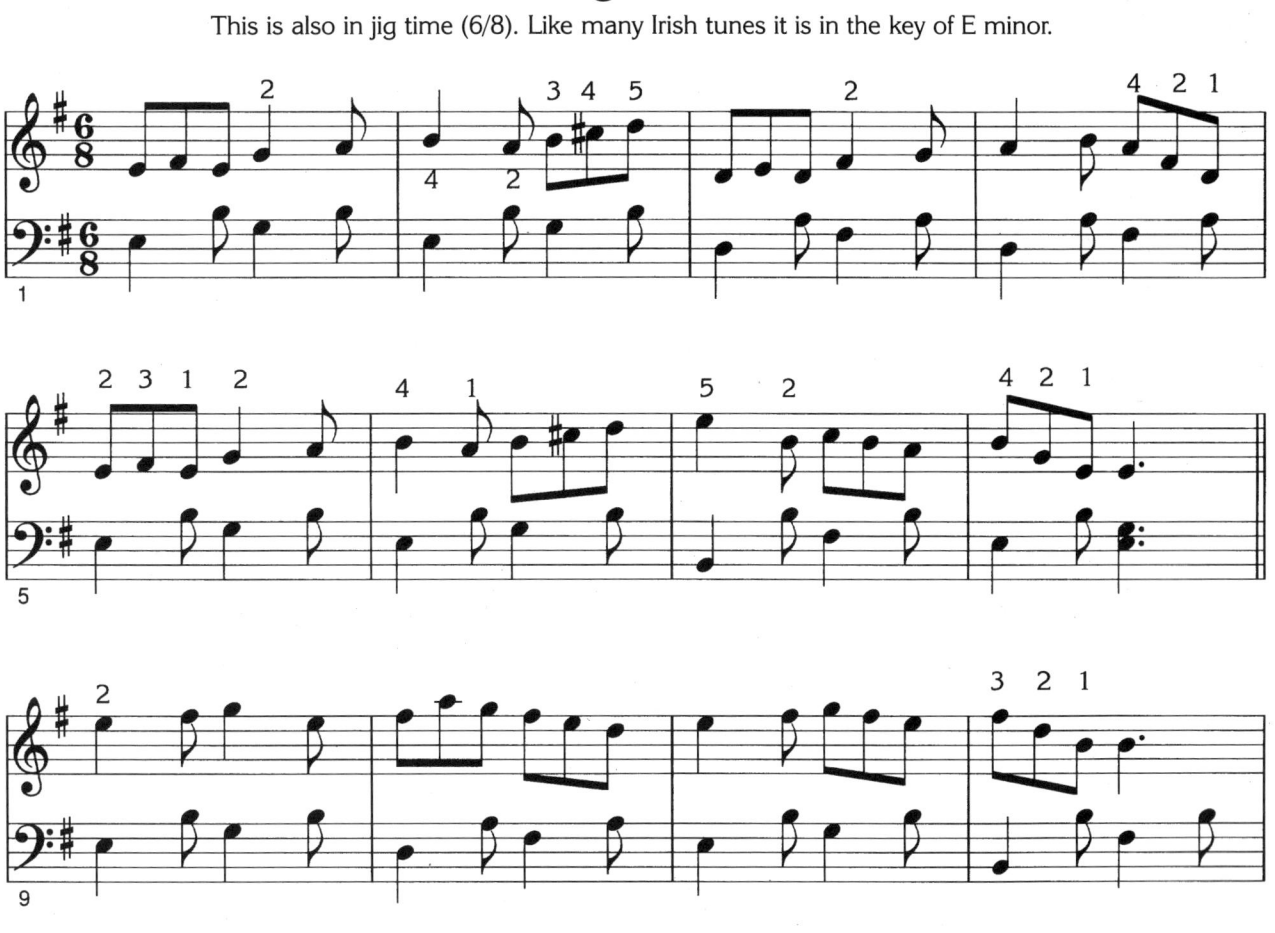

This is also in jig time (6/8). Like many Irish tunes it is in the key of E minor.

CHAPTER 2

The tunes in Chapter 1 were fairly simple, chosen to introduce you to a new style of piano playing. In this chapter you'll be attempting more difficult tunes. I will also introduce you to methods of ornamentation and variation. With experience you should be able to apply these techniques to tunes you choose yourself.

It is very important to realise that Irish traditional music like other folk musics is of an oral tradition. Music is learned and passed on by ear and without notation. This will be a difficult concept for many piano players, especially those of the classical tradition who rely on notation to learn their music. However, don't be disheartened. With practice and patience the dependency on the music will lessen.

Use the versions I've given as springboards. When you learn the tune close the book and do your own thing! Don't think that you're making a mistake if you don't play it exactly as I've written it.

A NOTE ON ORNAMENTATION

Ornamentation is used to enhance or embellish a tune. The ornaments must not dominate the tune itself. The rules applying to the ornamentation of tunes are the same for the piano as for other traditional instruments. Ornamentation applies only to the tune (the right hand) and not to the bass line. The most common ornaments for the piano are the "cut" and the "casadh".

TYPES OF ORNAMENT :

THE CUT
This is used to separate two notes of the same pitch.

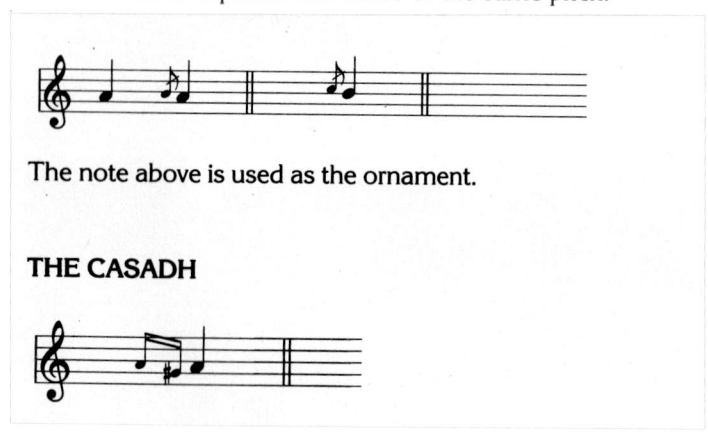

The note above is used as the ornament.

THE CASADH

I use the symbol ⌢ to represent the casadh. This is like a short roll - use the note a semitone below the note being ornamented (much like an inverted mordent). The long roll as used in other instruments sounds very cumbersome so I've chosen to exclude it. Anybody who plays traditional music on other instruments such as fiddle or tin whistle will notice that the notes used in the ornaments for the piano are different.

PATSY BRODERICK

Dónal na Gréine

Varying the Tune

Irish music is not by nature a written tradition. For generations the music has been passed on aurally. Nowadays, however, a great many musicians can read music, so quite often a tune is learned from staff notation. The aural nature of the music implies that changes will take place in the tune: nothing is fixed or permanent. The basics will be the same, but each time it is performed there will be subtle differences in phrasing, rhythm, ornamentation and sometimes even in the melody itself. Different versions of the same tune can be heard from region to region and quite often from player to player. It is important to remember that there is no such thing as one correct version of a tune. When studying Irish music, the more listening you do, the more you'll recognise and appreciate differences in style. When playing the piano the bass can also be varied. It is, however, the accompaniment to the tune, so keep it simple.

The first tune is **Dónal na Gréine**, a double jig. As with most tunes it is in two parts: eight bars in each part. I suggest that you become familiar with the tune in its basic form before introducing the ornamentation and certainly before tackling possible variations. This takes great patience but it is worth the effort.

Bars 1 and 2 (unvaried)

Bars 5 and 6, 1 and 2 can be varied thus:

OR

These are very simple changes but they create greater interest. The possibilities are endless.

Paddy Canny's Jig

(also known as 'Petticoat Loose)

I learned this tune from Paddy Canny, a fiddle player from East Clare. He played it with Peter O'Loughlin and Paddy Murphy, accompanied by Bridie Lafferty. The tune is unusual in that it modulates from the key of C to D and A minor. This is a double jig: each part is repeated.

Bars 1 and 2 can be varied thus:

Bars 3 and 4 can be varied thus:

GERALDINE COTTER

The Galway Rambler

This is a single reel: each part is played only once, with no repeats. Usually the tune is repeated three times. This reel is in the key of G.

Bars 3 and 4 can be varied thus:

OR

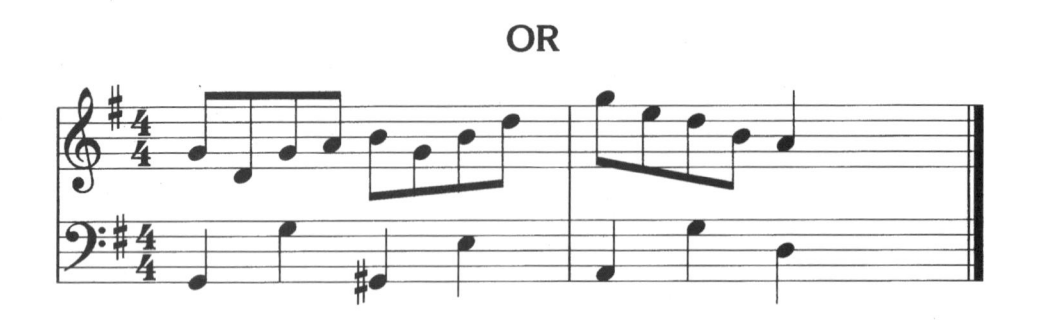

THE KILFENORA CÉILÍ BAND - WINNERS OF THE ALL-IRELAND CHAMPIONSHIP 1993, '94 AND '95.

Cooley's Reel

This tune is named after the famous accordion player Joe Cooley, late of Peterswell, Co. Galway. It is a double reel. The tune is in the lah mode (minor key).

Bars 3 and 4 can be varied thus:

Notice that the left hand moves in a scale passage. Bars 9 and 10 can be varied thus:

The possibilities are endless. Here are some more examples:

Bar 3:

Bar 9:

Bar 11:

Try these examples for the left hand:

Bar 2:

Bars 6, 7 and 8:

THE LIVERPOOL CÉILÍ BAND 1966, WITH PEGGY ATKINS ON PIANO. (NOTE ALSO CHARLIE LENNON ON FIDDLE, THIRD FROM RIGHT AT THE BACK.)

The Greencastle Hornpipe

Each part of this tune is repeated. It is in the key of G most of the time. (The second half uses some minor chords.)

Here are possible variations for the right hand.

Bar 6:

Bar 8 or 16:

Possible variations for 'The Greencastle Hornpipe' - left hand:

Bars 3 and 4

Bar 5

Bars 12 to 16

JOSEPHINE KEEGAN

Tatter Jack Walsh
This is a double jig in the key of D.

KEVIN TAYLOR, PIANO PLAYER WITH
THE THATCH CÉILÍ BAND IN LONDON.

Variations for the right hand - **Bars 1, 5 and 13:**

Bar 4:

Bar 9:

Some variations for the left hand

Bar 12:

Bars 15 and 16

This is a good variation when repeating the second half.

OR

Bars 15 and 16

Use this when leading back to the start of the tune.

OR

Bars 15 and 16

Geraldine Cotter's seinn an piano

CHAPTER 3

VAMPING

Vamping is a term used to describe the type of piano accompaniment used in traditional music. The tune is not played: chords are used instead - a single note or octave bass in the left hand and a chord in the right hand. The bass note (left hand) is played on the beat and the treble (right hand) plays on the off beat. A good piano accompanist, by tastefully combining the elements of rhythm and harmony, can enhance the playing of musicians. More players also like the support that good piano accompaniment can provide. However, this has to be done sensitively so that it doesn't become monotonous. In order to play well a good understanding of tunes is necessary. Knowledge of keys and chords is essential.

PLAYING WITH A CÉILÍ BAND

In a Céilí Band the main body of instruments plays the tune, the drum keeps the rhythm, and the piano provides the harmonic accompaniment as well as helping to maintain a rhythm.
1. Keep a steady rhythm.
2. An octave bass is generally preferable.
3. Make sure that the right hand (which generally plays the chords) is played lightly. Remember that the left hand plays on the beat so that if the right hand is too heavy a syncopated effect will result.
4. The drummer usually gives taps for the band to begin but sometimes it is the piano player who has this role. Kitty Linnane, founder member of the Kilfenora Céilí Band, had a unique style of introducing the tunes on the piano. This, in fact, was one of the hallmarks of this great band of the fifties. The "taps" are chords played (both hands together) in the key in which the tune is written:

[a] Two taps are played for a reel:

[b] Two taps are played for a jig

[c] Three taps are played for a hornpipe beginning on the last beat of the bar.

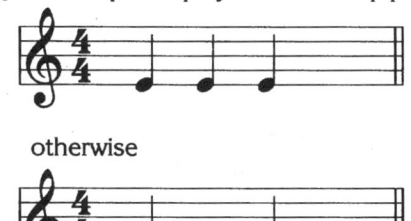

otherwise

This also applies to marches.

It is important to know the speed of the tune because the introductory taps on the drum or piano set the pace.

There are many excellent recordings of Céilí Bands available. Most bands have their own distinctive style. The piano player contributes to this. Here is a list of some of the more famous band piano players:

Kilfenora Band:	Kitty Linnane (R.I.P.)
Tulla Band:	George Byrt, Seán Reid (R.I.P.)
Liverpool Band:	Peggy Peakin, Peggy Atkins
Shaskeen Band:	Carl Hession, Geraldine Cotter
Moving Cloud:	Carl Hession
Templehouse Band:	Mary Corcoran
Castle Céilí Band:	Bridie Lafferty
Macalla:	Patsy Broderick
Naomh Eoin Céilí Band:	Ann Larkin
Disirt Tola Céilí Band:	Carol Talty

KITTY LINNANE

THE TULLA CÉILÍ BAND OF THE LATE 50S WITH GEORGE BYRT ON PIANO.

Accompanying Soloists or Smaller Groups

A more stylized approach can be adopted when accompanying smaller groups or soloists. A heavy bass line is not necessary. There can be more variety in the left hand as well as more movement in the right hand. Again a good knowledge of tunes is important. Tunes are chosen by bands primarily because of their suitability for dancing: they tend to be very rhythmic and have "lift". They can often be accompanied quite simply, using basic chords. While rhythm is a factor for all musicians it is not the only criterion used by solo musicians. Tunes are often chosen for their melodic appeal as well as rhythmic qualities. Quite often these tunes are unsuitable as band tunes.

This type of tune can be more complicated to accompany. Key changes can be more difficult. One of the best exponents of this style of playing is Charlie Lennon. He is also well known as a great fiddle player and composer. Not only does he choose nice chord progressions but has a very unique approach with his right hand. Check the discography for a list of his recordings. He has accompanied many musicians, including Frankie Gavin, Seamus Connolly and Paddy O'Brien. He has influenced many musicians, including myself.

A style of accompaniment which is lately gaining in popularity is from Cape Breton. Máire O'Keeffe and Donna Long show this influence in their piano playing.

CHARLIE LENNON

Another great piano player is Carl Hession. His style is also very distinctive. Like all good accompanists he approaches each tune differently, choosing chords which bring out the best in the piece. Carl is not alone a good pianist but is also a composer and arranger - see discography.

THE MOVING CLOUD CÉILÍ BAND WITH CARL HESSION ON PIANO.

FELIX DOLAN

Another favourite accompanist of mine is Felix Dolan. An American by birth, he has recorded widely with such greats as Joe Burke, Andy McGann and, more recently, with the great box player, Joe Derrane. His additional experience as a flute player enhances his skill as an accompanist.

There are many other pianists worth listening to: Brid Cranitch, Brian McGrath, Patsy Broderick, Bridie Lafferty, Josephine Keegan, Séamus Quinn, Mary Corcoran, Brendan Mac Eachrain and Maureen Glynn to name but a few (see discography).

MAUREEN GLYNN

BRID CRANITCH

EAMON AND GERALDINE COTTER

WHERE TO START
STEP 1: FORMING CHORDS FOR THE RIGHT HAND

Take any note e.g. C. Place the note a third (E) and a fifth (G) above it. You now have the chord of C major - CEG.

This is said to be in root position.

First inversion is when the third is at the bottom.

Second inversion is when the fifth is at the bottom.

The chords used to accompany a tune are based on the key of the piece ie. the scale on which the piece is based, eg. Scale of G:

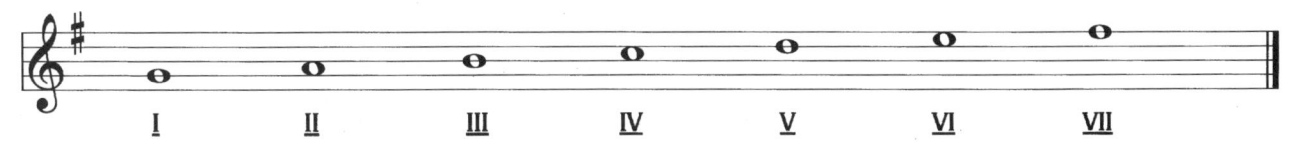

Chord I is based on G i.e. GBD
Chord II is based on A i.e. ACE
Chord III is based on B i.e. BDF# (F# is in the key signature)

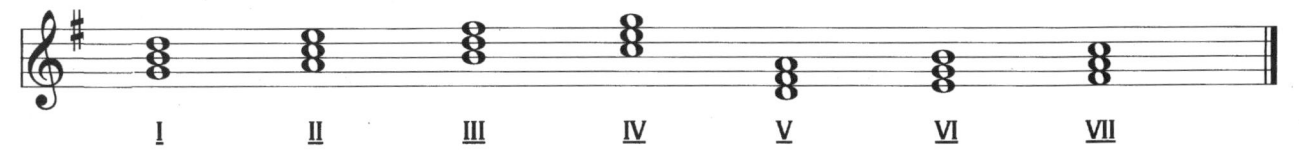

The same process applies to other keys. All these chords are in root position.
In Irish music the most commonly used chords are I, II, IV, V and VI. The most common keys are C, G, D, A, A minor, E minor and D minor - G and D being the more common.

Practise the following: chord I in all positions.
Apply this process to all other chords.

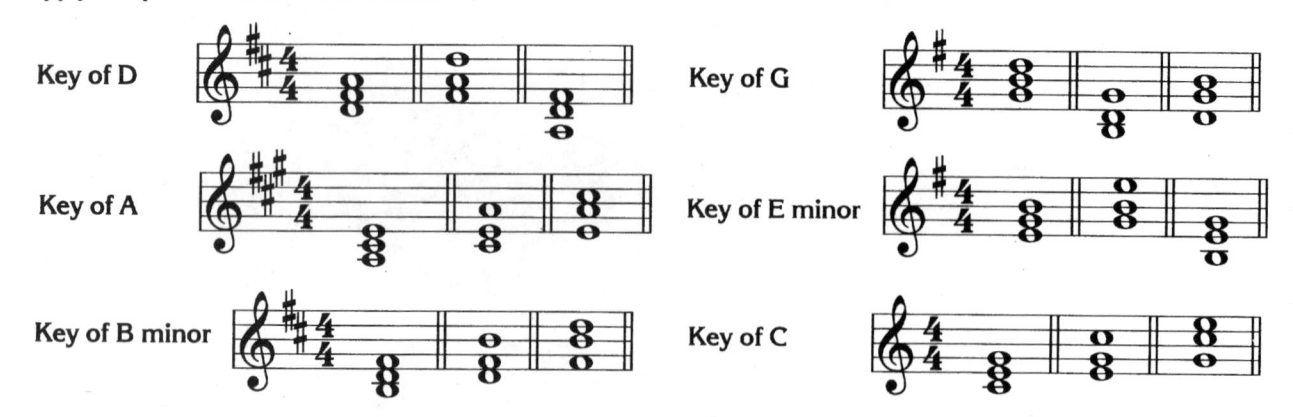

Key of D

Key of G

Key of A

Key of E minor

Key of B minor

Key of C

STEP 2: THE LEFT HAND

The left hand plays the note on which the chord is based. If the chord of G is being used, the left hand plays G; if chord D is used, a D is played by the left hand etc.

The left hand can also play the other notes of the chord but generally not on the first beat of the bar. The following are exercises which you can practise:

Vamping in Reel Time

Vamping in Jig Time

The rhythm of a jig is that of the words "Humpty Dumpty sat on a wall"
You can apply this to all the other keys.

STEP 3: PROGRESSING FROM ONE CHORD TO ANOTHER - SOME HINTS

Don't use two consecutive root position chords.
You may repeat the same chord.
Move to notes nearby.
Keep as many of the same notes as possible, eg.

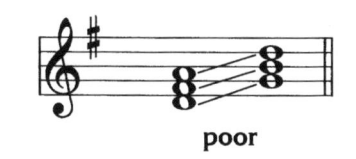

good   poor

Practise the following progressions:
   Moving from G to D

A common progression used in Irish music is **I, IV, V, I**:

This can also be played down an octave.

Practise the following extracts:

The Galway Rambler

Cooley's Reel

A 7th chord is formed when another 3rd above the 5th note is added e.g. GBDF.

I've used this chord in Bar 4 of 'The Mountain Top'.

THE TEMPLEHOUSE CÉILÍ BAND WITH MARY CORCORAN ON PIANO

Here is a complete tune to work on. Alternative bass notes are written underneath in letters.

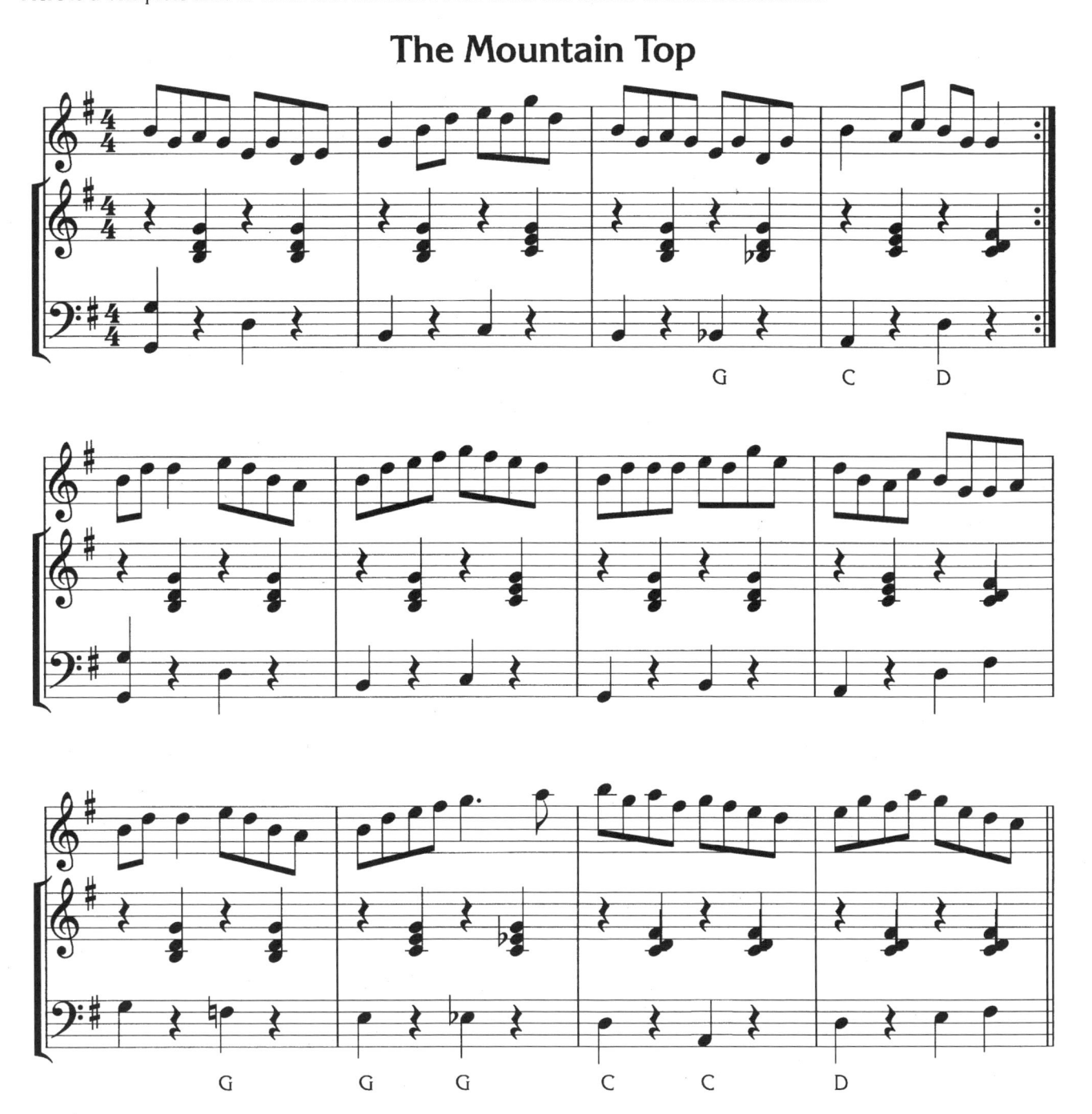

The Mountain Top

Notice the introduction of chromatic notes in the left hand - bars 2, 3, 4 and also bars 12, 13 and 14.

Varying the Accompaniment

There are many ways of varying the accompaniment. The most obvious way is to change the chords. As in the previous example scale passages or chromatic movement can be added. Rhythmic variation is also a possibility. So far we have kept rhythm fairly simple but try to experiment as you progress.

Notice that one of the notes of the chord is being held in the right hand.

THE TULLA CÉILÍ BAND WITH GEORGE BYRT ON PIANO.

OTHER KEYS

Sometimes musicians use instruments tuned in Eb - up a semitone from the more conventional D tuning. If, for example, a flute player plays an Eb flute, a tune in D sounds in Eb. A fiddle player can tune up a semitone, and the fingering doesn't change for the flautist, but the piano tuning is fixed. The pianist therefore has to transpose up a semitone. Knowledge of the keys of Eb, Bb, Ab, Db, Bb minor and F minor is needed.

Here are the chords of I, IV, and V in the above keys. Some of these can be transposed down an octave.

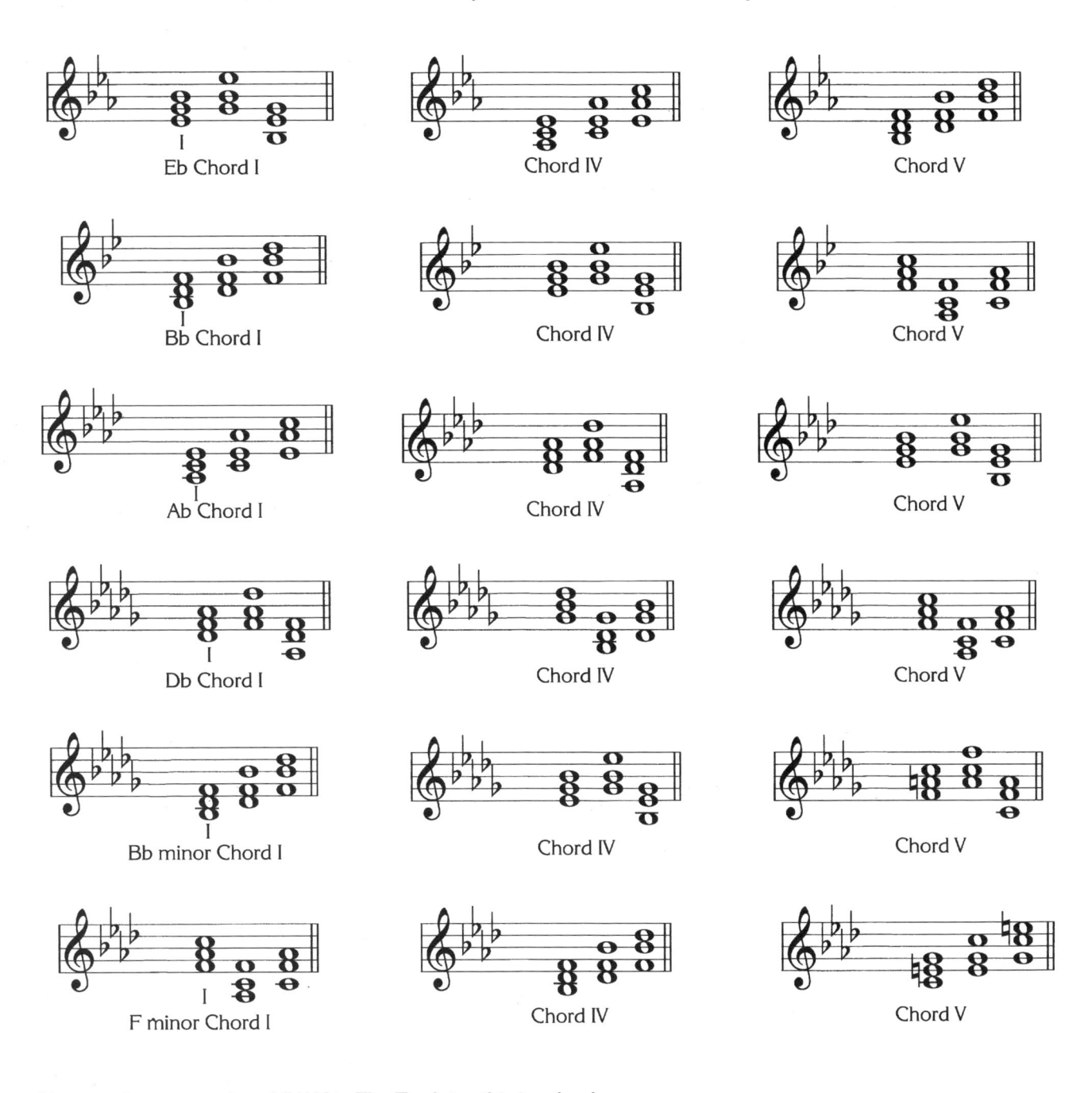

Eb Chord I — Chord IV — Chord V

Bb Chord I — Chord IV — Chord V

Ab Chord I — Chord IV — Chord V

Db Chord I — Chord IV — Chord V

Bb minor Chord I — Chord IV — Chord V

F minor Chord I — Chord IV — Chord V

Here are the progressions I-IV-V-I in Eb. Try doing this in other keys.

A Fig for a Kiss

Here is a slip jig in F minor. The harmony here is very simple. The tune itself is a single tune - each part (8 bars) played once.

In 9/8 time there are 3 dotted crotchets per bar. In the first version I have used one chord per bar. The right hand remains the same but a different position is used in the left hand. Now try some of the variations which are possible. These examples have a change of chord on the third beat.

Bars 1 to 3

Bar 9

Bars 9-11

Treat this chapter as an introduction to vamping. Listen to recordings to develop your knowledge of tunes and styles. With experience and good listening your playing will develop.

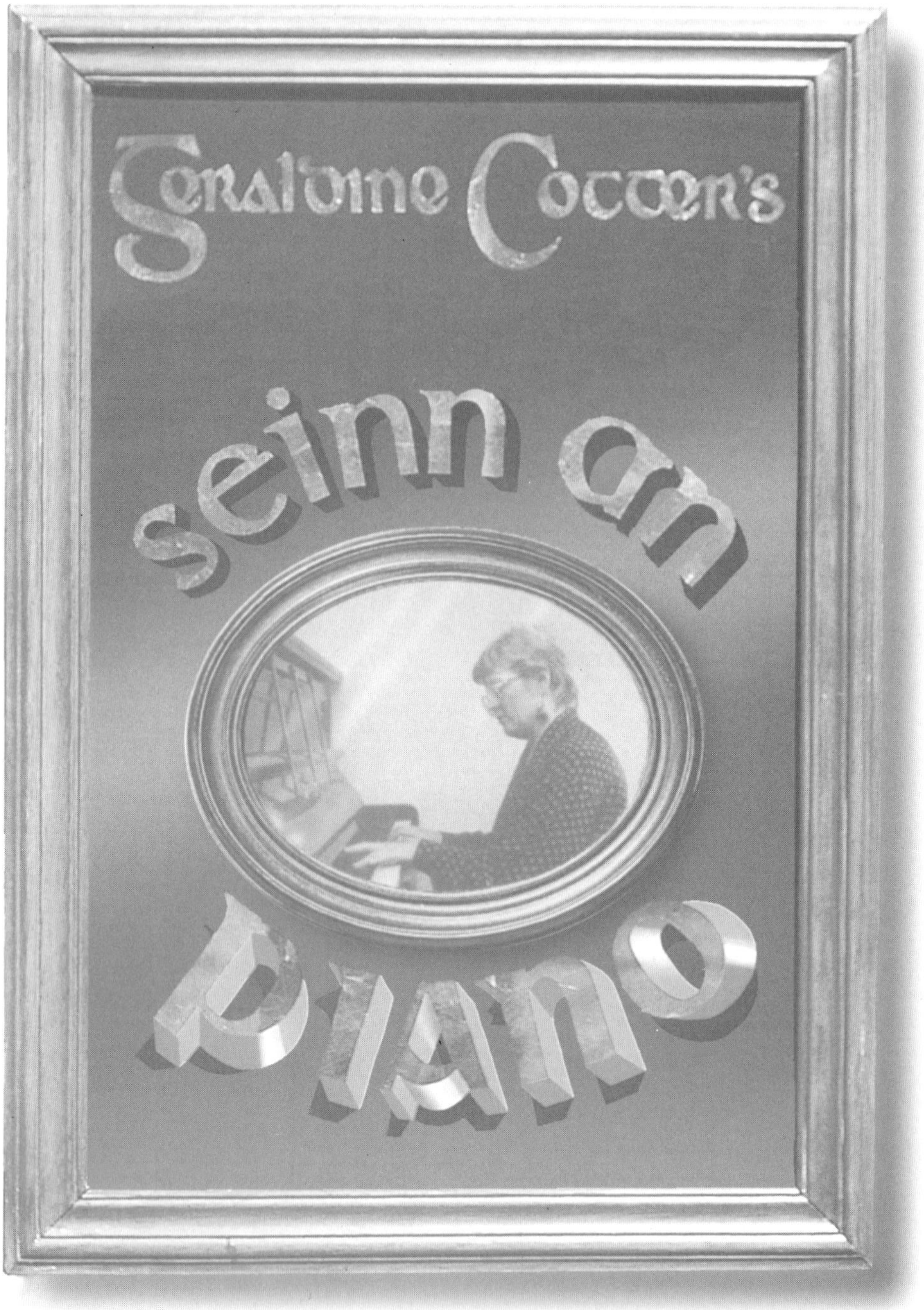
Geraldine Cotter's
seinn an
piano

CHAPTER 4

Dance Tunes

Tune	Page
Ace and Deuce of Pipering, The **(Set Dance)**	64
Austin Barrett's **(Jig)**	48
Ballyvourney (also known as Lackagh Cross) **(Polka)**	70
Caisleáin an Óir **(Hornpipe)**	61
Cuckoo's Nest, The **(Hornpipe)**	63
Peggy on the Settle **(Reel)**	54
Eileen Curran **(Reel)**	55
Ewe Reel, The **(Reel)**	59
Fahy's Reel	53
Gander in the Pratie Hole, The **(Jig)**	52
Gillian's Apples **(Jig)**	49
Hunt, The **(Set Dance)**	65
Jenny Picking Cockles **(Reel)**	56
Job of Journeywork, The **(Set Dance)**	67
Johnny Mickey's **(Polka)**	68
Lodge Road, The **(Set Dance)**	66
Lucky in Love **(Reel)**	58
Mulqueeney's **(Hornpipe)**	60
Pay the Reckoning **(Jig)**	50
Rose in the Heather **(Jig)**	51
Scotch Mary **(Reel)**	57
Toureengarbh Glen **(Polka)**	69
Wicklow Hornpipe, The	62

Jigs
Austin Barrett's

Gillian's Apples

Pay the Reckoning

Rose in the Heather

The Gander in the Pratie Hole

Reels
Fahy's Reel

This is a composition of the East Galway fiddle player Paddy Fahy

Peggy on the Settle

Eileen Curran

Jenny Picking Cockles

Scotch Mary

Lucky in Love

The Ewe Reel

HORNPIPES
Mulqueeney's

Caisleáin an Óir

This tune was written by Junior Crehan, the famous Clare musician.

The Wicklow Hornpipe

The Cuckoo's Nest

SET DANCES
The Ace and Deuce of Pipering

The Hunt

The Lodge Road

The Job of Journeywork

POLKAS
Johnny Mickey's

Toureengarbh Glen

Ballyvourney
(also known as Lackagh Cross)

BIBLIOGRAPHY

The following is a list of Irish Music books of general interest. Not all deal specifically with piano music.

Breathnach, B.B.: FOLK MUSIC AND DANCES OF IRELAND Ossian Publications 1971/1996

Bunting, Edward: THE ANCIENT MUSIC OF IRELAND Vols. 1-3, Waltons Manufacturing Ltd. Dublin, 1969.

BUNTING'S ANCIENT MUSIC OF IRELAND ed. Donal O'Sullivan with Mícheál O Súilleabháin, Cork University Press.

Crofts, T.M.: DANCE MUSIC OF IRELAND, Waltons Manufacturing Ltd.

Curtis, P.J.: NOTES FROM THE HEART, Torc 1994

Lennon, Charlie: MUSICAL MEMORIES World Music Publications, Dublin 1993.

O Canainn, T.: TRADITIONAL MUSIC IN IRELAND, Republished by Ossian Publications Ltd. Cork, 1994.

O'Neill, Francis: IRISH FOLK MUSIC, A FASCINATING HOBBY, Chicago 1910

IRISH MINSTRELS AND MUSICIANS Mercier Press, Cork 1987.

WAIFS AND STRAYS OF GAELIC MELODY, Mercier Press Cork, 1980.

POPULAR SELECTIONS FROM O'NEILL'S DANCE MUSIC OF IRELAND
Waltons Manufacturing Ltd. Dublin, 1969.

Ó Riada, Seán: OUR MUSICAL HERITAGE, Dolmen Press 1982.

Petrie, G.: ANCIENT MUSIC OF IRELAND, Republished by Gregg International, 1988.

Reavy, Ed: WHERE THE SHANNON RISES, Dal gCais Publications ISSN 0790 7303.

Ward, John J.: DANCE MUSIC OF IRELAND

THE JOURNAL OF CLARE No. 7 1984, Dal gCais Publications

THE JOURNAL OF CLARE No. 9 1988, Dal gCais Publications

* For an up to date list of publications by Ossian write to
  Ossian Publications
  P.O. Box 84, Cork, Ireland
  email: ossian@iol.ie
  web: ossian.ie

DISCOGRAPHY

Geraldine Cotter:
Piano+ (Geraldine's solo recording): GC001
SHASKEEN LIVE VOL. 1: CFA3506
SHASKEEN LIVE VOL. 2: CFA3507
Piano - **Geraldine Cotter**
For more information on Shaskeen recordings, contact Eamon Cotter, Balleen, Kilmaley, Co. Clare.
Eamon Cotter - solo flute with piano accompaniment by Geraldine Cotter. (CDEC001)

Mícheál O Súilleabháin:
OILEÁN/ISLAND: Venture, TCVE/CDVE40
CASADH/TURNING: Venture, TCVE/CDVE904
GAISEADH/FLOWING: Venture, TCVE/CDVE915
THE DOLPHIN'S WAY: Venture, TCVE/CDVE1
CRY OF THE MOUNTAIN: Gael-Linn CEFC079
MÍCHEÁL O SÚILLEABHÁIN: Gael-Linn CEFC/CEFCD046 (A Variety of Keyboard Instruments).

Seán Ó Riada:
Ó RIADA'S FAREWELL: Claddagh CC12
REACHARACHT AN RIADAIGH: Gael-Linn CEFC010
PLAYBOY OF THE WESTERN WORLD: Gael-Linn CEFC012
Ó RIADA SA GAIETY: Gael-Linn CEFC/CEFCD027
SEÁN Ó RIADA: Gael-Linn CEFC/CEFCD032
SEÁN Ó RIADA, SEÁN Ó SÉ, CEOLTÓIRÍ CHUALANN: Gael-Linn CEFC016
NA CÉIRNÍNÍ 45 - SEÁN Ó RIADA, SEÁN Ó SÉ, CEOLTÓIRÍ CHUALANN: Gael-Linn CEFC076

Charlie Lennon:
UP AND AWAY/ CROCH SUAS É: CEFC/CEFCD103 (Frankie Gavin, flute)
ÓMOS DO JOE COOLEY: CEFC/CEFCD115 (Frankie Gavin, Paul Brock)
MUSICAL MEMORIES: WOMMC/WOMCD101.
FRANKIE GOES TO TOWN BKC/KCD001(Frankie Gavin, fiddle)
CAROUSEL Seamus & Manus McGuire Gael Linn CEFC/CEFCD 105
THE BANKS OF THE SHANNON (Paddy O'Brien, Seamus Connolly) CL40

Bridie Lafferty:
PADDY CANNY, P.J. HAYES, PETER O'LOUGHLIN: Shamrock Records Harp10.
Joe Cooley CÓIPCHEART: CEFC/CEFCD044
CASTLE CÉILÍ BAND: CL5

Carl Hession:
CEOL INNÉ CEOL INNIU - music arranged, composed and played by Carl Hession, accompanied by other musicians including Máirtín O'Connor, Steve Cooney, Dermot Byrne and Frankie Gavin. Gael Linn CEFC/CEFCD 173.
THE BEST OF FRANKIE GAVIN RTEMC/RTECD 187
MOVING CLOUD CÉILÍ BAND Green Linnet CSIF/GLCD 1150
MO CHÁIRDÍN Paul Brock Gael Linn CEFC/CEFCD 155
GREEN GROVES OF ERIN Shaskeen VRL 5001
THE SHASKEEN BRL 4053

Felix Dolan:
A Tribute to Michael Coleman (with Joe Burke & Andy McGann) Green Linnet CSIF/GLCD 3097
JOE BURKE, ANDY MCGANN, FELIX DOLAN Shanachie SH29012
GIVE US ANOTHER Joe Derrane Green Linnet CSIF/GLCD 1149

Bríd Cranitch:
ÉISTIGH SEAL (accompanying Matt Cranitch - fiddle) Gael Linn CEFC104
TAKE A BOW (accompanying Matt Cranitch - fiddle) Ossian OSS 5/OSSCD 5
GIVE IT SHTICK (accompanying Matt Cranitch - fiddle) Ossian OSS 6
A SMALL ISLAND - TRADITIONAL MUSIC FROM CORK (with Vince Milne, fiddle and Pat Sullivan, accordion)
 Ossian OSS 70/OSSCD 70

Seán Maguire accompanied on piano by **Josephine Keegan**
SEÁN MAGUIRE - BEST OF IRISH TRADITIONAL MUSIC: Outlet COX 1002
SEÁN MAGUIRE - CHAMPION IRISH TRADITIONAL FIDDLER: Outlet COX 1005
SEÁN MAGUIRE - Josephine Keegan playing solo piano on the track 'THE BEE'S WING' Viva VV103

Paddy Glackin with Jolyon Jackson (keyboards, synthesisers)
HIDDEN GROUND: Tara TA2009.

Kevin Burke with Paul Brady, piano:
IF THE CAP FITS: Mulligan CLUN/LUNCD021 (Europe); Green Linnet GLCD3009 (US)
EAVESDROPPER: Mulligan CLUN/LUNCD039 (Europe); Green Linnet GLCD3002 (US)

John Roe and Kevin Boyle
LE CHÉILE ARÍS: Inchecronin 7423.

The Bothy Band (with Tríona Ní Dhomhnaill on Keyboards):
THE BOTHY BAND 1975: Mulligan CLUN/LUNCD002 (Europe); GLCD3011 (US)
OLD HAG YOU HAVE KILLED ME: Mulligan CLUN/LUNCD007 (Europe); GLCD3005 (US)
AFTERHOURS: Mulligan CLUN/LUNCD030 (Europe); GLCD3016 (US)
OUT OF THE WIND, INTO THE SUN: Mulligan CLUN/LUNCD013 (Europe); GLCD3013 (US)

Ardady (with Patsy Broderick, piano)
AFTER THE BALL Dara DARAC/DARACD 037
Many Happy Returns Shanachie SH/SHCD 79095

CEOL TIGH NEACHTAIN: Music from Galway (piano by Patsy Broderick): Gael-Linn CEFC/CEFCD145.

IRISH MUSIC FROM THE FAVOURITE: Originally released on Leader LED2051, reissued on cassette as PADDY IN THE SMOKE (OSS19) by Ossian Publications in 1989

JOHN MCGETTIGAN AND HIS IRISH MINSTRELS: Topic 12T367

IRISH DANCE MUSIC: Collected by Reg Hall. Folkways Records, FW8821.
IRISH DANCE MUSIC: - second edition of the above, containing a revised selection of recordings taken from 78rpm records, and new notes. Topic TSCD602

DAN SULLIVAN'S SHAMROCK BAND: Topic 12T366

Séamus Connolly: NOTES FROM MY MIND Green Linnet CSIF/GLCD 1087 (piano by Helen Kisiel and Tríona Ní Dhomhnaill.

Mary MacNamara: TRADITIONAL MUSIC FROM EAST CLARE (piano by Séamus Quinn) Claddagh 4CC60/CC60CD

John Carty and Brian McGrath: THE CAT THAT ATE THE CANDLE CIC/CICD 099

JAMES MORRISON AND TOM ENNIS - piano by John Muller, Ed Geoghegan & Clare Reardon: Topic 12T390

FLUTERS OF OLD ERIN - Various piano players: Viva Voce 002

James Morrison 'THE PROFESSOR': Viva Voce 001.

WILLIAM MULALLY AND ED LEE Viva Voce 005

KILFENORA CÉILÍ BAND (piano by Fintan MacMahon) GTDHHC/GTDHHCD 141

Chris Droney 'THE FERTILE ROCK' with George Byrt on piano CIC110

Máire O'Keeffe 'CÓISIR - HOUSE PARTY' Gael Linn CEFC/CEFCD 165

Liz Carroll 'A FRIEND INDEED' accompanied by Martin Fahey: Shanachie SH29013.

JOSEPHINE MARSH accordion music with Jim Higgins on piano JMMC 001/JMCD001

GALWAY TO DUBLIN - some solo piano by Eleanor Kane Rounder RRCD1087

Many of the recordings made by the musicians mentioned in the introduction are now out of print, but look out for reissues.

Comhaltas Ceoltóirí Éireann also produce a range of recordings. For more details write to Comhaltas Ceoltóirí Éireann, Belgrave Square, Monkstown, Co. Dublin.

Photo Credits and Sources

Ballinakill Band - Courtesy of Sr. Benedict Moylan
Bríd Cranitch - Courtesy of Bríd Cranitch
Bridie Lafferty - Mick O'Connor
Charlie Lennon - Courtesy of Charlie Lennon
Ed Reavy - from 'Where the Shannon Rises' © 1971 Joseph Reavy
Eleanor Kane - Courtesy of Eileen and Liz Carroll
Felix Dolan - Courtesy of Felix Dolan
Frank Lee - Comhaltas Ceoltóirí Éireann
Geraldine Cotter - John Kelly, Clare Champion
Jimmy Power, Reg Hall & Tony Ledwith - Courtesy of Reg Hall
John Kimmel/Joe Linder - 'John Kimmel - Virtuoso of the Irish Accordion' Smithsonian Folkways LP RF112
Kevin Taylor - Courtesy of Reg Hall
Kilfenora Céilí Band p. 11 - Courtesy of Sr. Benedict Moylan
Kilfenora Céilí Band p. 24 - Courtesy of John Lynch; photo by Christy MacNamara
Kincora Céilí Band - 'Ceol Tíre' Comhaltas Ceoltóirí Éireann LP
Kitty Linnane - John Kelly, Clare Champion
Maureen Glynn - Courtesy of Maureen Glynn
Mícheál Ó Súilleabháin - Courtesy of Colm Henry
Moving Cloud - Courtesy of Paul Brock
Patsy Broderick - from 'Ceol Tigh Neachtain' Gael Linn CEFC/CEFCD 145
Seán Ó Riada - from 'The Achievement of Seán Ó Riada' edited by Bernard Harris and
    Grattan Freyer, 1981, Irish Humanity Centre & Keohanes
Templehouse Céilí Band - Courtesy of Mary Corcoran
Tulla Céilí Band p. 11 - Courtesy of Sr. Benedict Moylan
Tulla Céilí Band p. 34 - Courtesy of Peggy & P.J. Hayes
Tulla Céilí Band p. 42 - Courtesy of Peggy & P.J. Hayes

Piano+
Geraldine's solo recording of
Irish music on the Piano & Tin Whistle.
GC001

Geraldine Cotter
Gortmore, Ennis, Co. Clare
Tel +353 (0)65 6821601
email: geraldinecotter.ennis@eircom.net
web: www.geraldinecotter.com

Ossian Publications produce and distribute a large range of traditional music
in book form, CD and video.
For an up-to-date list of all our products please send us your name and address.

Ossian Publications, P.O. Box 84, Cork, Ireland.
Phone: 353-(0)21-4502040
Fax: 353-(0)21-4502025

e-mail: ossian@iol.ie
web: www.ossian.ie